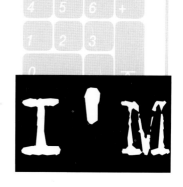

I'M BUSY NOW

Can I ignore you

some other time?

D0326788

Never walk down the hall without a document in your hands.
People with documents in their hands look like hardworking employees heading for important meetings. People with nothing in their hands look like they're heading for the cafeteria. People with the newspaper in their hands look like they're heading for the bathroom. Above all, make sure you carry loads of stuff home with you at night, thus generating the false impression that you work longer hours than you do.

LEAVE ME ALONE
I'M NOT BEING RUDE

YOU'RE JUST INSIGNIFICANT

A pat on the back is a breath away from a
kick in the pants.

Don't be irreplaceable — if you can't be replaced,
you can't be promoted.

The more crap you put up with, the more crap you
are going to get.

Eat one live toad the first thing in the morning and
nothing worse will happen to you the rest of the day.

When the bosses talk about improving productivity,
they are never talking about themselves.

If at first you don't succeed, try again. Then quit.
No use being a damn fool about it.

There will always be beer cans rolling on the floor
of your car when the boss asks for a ride home from
the office.

Everything can be filed under 'miscellaneous.'

Never delay the ending of a meeting or the beginning
of a cocktail hour.

Anyone can do any amount of work provided it isn't
the work he is supposed to be doing.

Never ask two questions in a business letter.
The reply will discuss the one you are least interested
in, and say nothing about the other.

THIS ISN'T AN OFFICE

It's hell with fluorescent lighting

Put decaf in the coffee maker for three weeks.

Once everyone has withdrawn from caffeine addiction, switch to espresso.

I PRETEND TO WORK

THEY PRETEND TO PAY ME

Find out where your boss shops and buy exactly the same outfits.
Wear them one day after your boss does.
This is especially effective if your boss is of a different gender than you.

I CAN ONLY PLEASE ONE PERSON EACH DAY

Today is not your day

Tomorrow doesn't look good either

THE NEXT TIME YOU GET A REJECTION LETTER FROM A PROSPECTIVE EMPLOYER OR PUBLISHER, JUST SEND THEM THE FOLLOWING:

Dear *[name of the person who signed the rejection letter]*,

Thank you for your letter of *[date of the rejection letter]*. **After careful consideration, I regret to inform you that I am unable to accept your refusal to offer me** *[employment with your firm/a contract to publish my book]*.

This year I have been particularly fortunate in receiving an unusually large number of rejection letters. With such a varied and promising field of candidates, it is impossible for me to accept all refusals. Despite *[name of the company or agency that sent you this letter]***'s outstanding qualifications and previous experience in rejecting** *[applicants/manuscripts]*, **I find that your rejection does not meet with my needs at this time. Therefore, I will initiate** *[employment/publishing]* **with your firm immediately following** *[graduation/job change, etc. -- get creative here]*. **I look forward to working with you.**

Best of luck in rejecting future *[candidates/manuscripts]*.

Sincerely,

[your name]

I LOVE
DEADLINES

I especially like the sound they make as they go whooshing by

WORKER DEAD AT DESK FOR 5 DAYS

Bosses of a publishing firm are trying to work out why no one noticed that one of their employees had been sitting dead at his desk for FIVE DAYS before anyone asked if he was feeling okay.

George Turklebaum, 51, who had been employed as a proof-reader at a New York firm for 30 years, had a heart attack in the open-plan office he shared with 23 other workers. He quietly passed away on Monday, but nobody noticed until Saturday morning when an office cleaner asked why he was still working during the weekend.

His boss Elliot Wachiaski said: "George was always the first guy in each morning and the last to leave at night, so no one found it unusual that he was in the same position all that time and didn't say anything. He was always absorbed in his work and kept much to himself."
A post-mortem examination revealed that he had been dead for five days after suffering a coronary. Ironically, George was proofreading manuscripts of medical textbooks when he died... You may want to give your co-workers a nudge occasionally.

Birmingham Sunday Mercury 07/01/2001

I DON'T

GET EVEN

I GET ODDER

DOUBLE STANDARDS

When I please my boss, I'm ass-kissing.

When my boss pleases his boss, he's co-operating.

When I take a long time, I am slow.

When my boss takes a long time, he is thorough.

When I don't do it, I am lazy.

When my boss doesn't do it, he is too busy.

When I do something without being told, I am trying to be smart.

When my boss does the same, that is initiative.

When I do good, my boss never remembers.

When I do wrong, he never forgets.

IN A MEETING

THE PRACTICAL ALTERNATIVE TO WORK

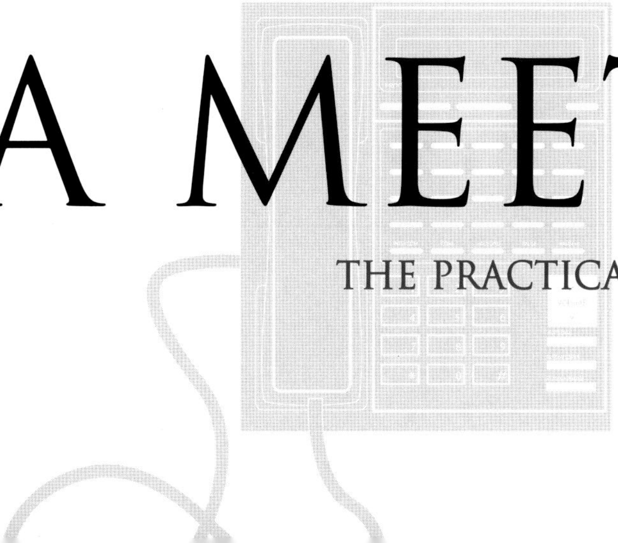

Grant me the serenity to accept the things I cannot change,
The courage to change the things I cannot accept,
And the wisdom to hide the bodies of those people
I had to kill today because they p----d me off...
Help me to be careful
Of the toes I step on today as they
May be connected to the hind end
That I may have to kiss tomorrow...!

TO ERR IS HUMAN

To forgive

is against company policy

TOP 10 REASONS TO GO TO WORK NAKED

1. Your boss is always yelling, "I wanna see your butt in here by 8:00!"

2. Take advantage of computer monitor radiation to work on your tan.

3. Inventive way to finally meet that hunk/babe in Human Resources.

4. I'd love to chip in, but I left my wallet in my pants.

5. To stop those creepy guys in Marketing from looking down your blouse.

6. You want to see if it's like the dream.

7. People stop stealing your pens after they've seen where you keep them.

8. Diverts attention from the fact that you also came to work drunk.

9. Gives 'bad hair day' a whole new meaning.

10. No one steals your chair.

TELL ME AGAIN
HOW LUCKY I AM
TO WORK HERE

I keep forgetting

THINGS TO SAY IF CAUGHT SLEEPING AT YOUR DESK

- They told me at the blood bank this might happen.

- Damn! Why did you interrupt me? I had almost figured out a solution to our biggest problem.

- Someone must've put decaf in the wrong pot.

- Whew! Guess I left the top off the White-Out! You probably got here just in time!

- I wasn't sleeping! I was meditating on the mission statement and envisioning a new paradigm.

- I was testing my keyboard for drool resistance.

- I was doing Yoga exercises to relieve work-related stress.

- This is just a 15-minute power nap as described in that time management course you sent me.

- The coffee machine is broken...

SITUATION

DESPERATE!

SEND CHOCOLATE

Send an e-mail to the rest of the company telling them exactly what you're doing.
For example: If anyone needs me, I'll be in the bathroom.

Page yourself over the intercom. Don't disguise your voice.

CHAOS, PANIC
& DISORDER

MY WORK HERE IS DONE

Get a greeting card that plays an insidious tune.

Wrap the musical chip in lots of cotton balls to make it
quiet and tape it underneath your victim's desk.
Act like he's crazy when he asks you if you hear music.

HARD WORK NEVER KILLED ANYONE

But why chance it?

GREAT EXCUSES FOR MONDAY MORNING

If it is all the same to you, I won't be coming in to work. The voices told me to clean all the guns today.

When I got up this morning, I took two Ex-Lax in addition to my Prozac. I can't get off the john, but I feel good about it.

My stigmata are acting up.

I can't come in to work today because I'll be stalking my previous boss, who fired me for not showing up for work. OK?

I am stuck in the blood pressure machine down at the Food Giant.

Yes, I seem to have contracted some attention-deficit disorder and who are you please?

Constipation has made me a walking time bomb.

I just found out that I was switched at birth. Legally, I shouldn't come to work knowing my employee records may now contain false information.

The psychiatrist said it was an excellent session. He even gave me this jaw restraint so I won't bite things when I am startled.

The dog ate my car keys. We're going to hitchhike to the vet and give her eternal peace. One day should do it.

I can't come to work today because the EPA has determined that my house is completely surrounded by wetlands and I have to arrange for helicopter transportation.

CONFESSION IS GOOD FOR THE SOUL

but bad for your career

You are more likely to be killed by a piece of office equipment than to win the lottery

ZERO MONDAY
ZERO TUESDAY
40% WEDNESDAY
20% THURSDAY
50% FRIDAY

ALWAYS
GIVE 100%
AT WORK

ALWAYS GIVE 100% AT WORK

12%	MONDAY
23%	TUESDAY
40%	WEDNESDAY
20%	THURSDAY
5%	FRIDAY

Put an official-looking sign over the control pad of your office fax or copy machine that says it is now voice-activated.

The sign should direct the users to say their full name in a loud, crisp voice (for tracking purposes, of course) followed by the desired commands, e.g., 'This is Bruce Smith, give me ten copies, no staple.'

IF AT FIRST YOU DON'T SUCCEED

DESTROY ALL EVIDENCE THAT YOU EVEN TRIED

RESUME MISTAKES

Reasons for Leaving Previous Job:

- Responsibility makes me nervous.

- They insisted that all employees get to work by 8:45 every morning. Couldn't work under those conditions.

- Note: Please don't misconstrue my 14 jobs as 'job-hopping'. I have never quit a job.

- Was met with a string of broken promises and lies, as well as cockroaches.

- I was working for my mom until she decided to move.

- The company made me a scapegoat - just like my three previous employers.

BAD DAY IN PROGRESS

Approach at

your own risk

VOICE MAIL

Never answer your phone if you have voice mail.
People don't call you just because they want to give you something for nothing — they call because they want YOU to do work for THEM. That's the way to live. Screen all your calls through voice mail. If somebody leaves a voice mail message for you and it sounds like impending work, respond during lunch hour. That way, you're hardworking and conscientious even though you're being a devious weasel.

If you diligently employ the method of screening incoming calls and then returning calls when nobody is there, this will greatly increase the odds that they will give up or look for a solution that doesn't involve you. The sweetest voice mail message you can ever hear is: 'Ignore my last message. I took care of it.' If your voice mailbox has a limit on the number of messages it can hold, make sure you reach that limit frequently. One way to do that is to never erase any incoming messages. If that takes too long, send yourself a few messages. Your callers will hear a recorded message that says, 'Sorry, this mailbox is full' — a sure sign that you are a hardworking employee in high demand.

I'M OUT OF MY MIND

but feel free to leave a message

MORE RESUME MISTAKES

Personal Qualities

- I'm married with 9 children. I don't require prescription drugs.

- I am extremely loyal to my present firm, so please don't let them know of my immediate availability.

- Number of dependents: 40.

- Marital Status: Often. Children: Various.

- I was proud to win the Gregg Typting Award.

- Please call me after 5:30 because I am self-employed and my employer does not know I am looking for another job.

I CAN SEE

YOUR POINT

BUT I STILL THINK YOU'RE FULL OF CRAP

Use computers to look busy. Any time you use a computer, it looks like work to the casual observer. You can send and receive personal e-mail, calculate your finances and generally have a blast without doing anything remotely related to work. These aren't exactly the societal benefits that everybody from the computer revolution expected but they're not bad either.

When you get caught by your boss — and you will get caught — your best defense is to claim you're teaching yourself to use the new software, thus saving valuable training funds. You're not a loafer, you're a self-starter. Offer to show your boss what you learned. That will make your boss scurry away like a frightened salamander.

I'LL TRY
BEING NICER

IF YOU TRY BEING SMARTER

Using the conferencing feature of your office phone, dial one person, then while it's ringing dial another and conference them together. Put your own phone on mute and listen to see how long they'll make small talk before figuring out that neither one placed the call.

IF YOU STAY CALM WHILST ALL AROUND YOU IS CHAOS

... then you probably haven't understood

the seriousness of the situation

Send e-mail messages saying there's free pizza or donuts or cake in the lunchroom. When people drift back to work complaining that they found none, lean back, pat your stomach and say, 'Oh you've got to be faster than that.'

HARD WORK NEVER KILLS ANYONE

who's supervising

MORE RESUME MISTAKES

- Here are my qualifications for you to overlook.
- Education: College, August 1880-May 1984.
- Work Experience: Dealing with customers' conflicts that arouse.
- Develop and recommend an annual operating expense fudget.
- I'm a rabid typist.
- Instrumental in ruining entire operation for a Midwest chain operation.

IF YOUR REQUEST IS

**REALLY** **URGENT**

I WOULD HAVE DONE IT ALREADY

Keep a messy desk. Top management can get away with a clean desk. For the rest of us, it looks like you're not working hard enough. Build huge piles of documents around your workspace.

To the observer, last year's work looks the same as today's work; it's volume that counts. Pile them high and wide. If you know somebody is coming to your cubicle, bury the document you'll need halfway down in an existing stack and rummage for it when they arrive.

WATCH OUT

OUT

WHATEVER HITS THE FAN WILL NOT BE DISTRIBUTED EVENLY

YOU KNOW YOU'RE TOO STRESSED WHEN

- You can achieve a 'runner's high' by sitting up.
- The sun is too loud.
- Antacid tablets become your sole source of nutrition.
- **You discover the esthetic beauty of office supplies.**
- You say the same sentence over and over again, not realizing that you've said it before.
- **You say the same sentence over and over again, not realizing that you've said it before.**

ALWAYS BE 100% BEHIND YOUR BOSS

Then it's easier

to stab him in the back

LAWS OF WORK

- When you don't know what to do, walk fast and look worried.

- You will always get the greatest recognition for the job you least like.

- No one gets sick on Wednesdays.

- **When confronted by a difficult problem you can solve it more easily by reducing it to the question, 'How would the Lone Ranger handle this?'**

- The longer the title, the less important the job.

- **Machines that have broken down will work perfectly when the repairman arrives.**

- An 'acceptable' level of employment means that the government economist to whom it is acceptable still has a job.

- Once a job is fouled up, anything done to improve it makes it worse.

- All vacations and holidays create problems, except for one's own.

PLEASE FILE ALL URGENT REQUESTS UNDER B

for bullshit

Personnel directors' unusual experiences interviewing prospective employees.

- A job applicant challenged the interviewer to an arm wrestle.

- Interviewee wore a Walkman, explaining that she could listen to the interviewer and the music at the same time.

- Candidate fell and broke an arm during the interview.

- Candidate announced she hadn't had lunch and proceeded to eat a hamburger and french fries in the interviewer's office.

- Candidate explained that her long-term goal was to replace the interviewer.

- Candidate said he never finished high school because he was kidnapped and kept in a closet in Mexico.

- Balding candidate excused himself and returned to the office a few minutes later wearing a headpiece.

- Applicant said if he was hired he would demonstrate his loyalty by having the corporate logo tattooed on his forearm.

- Applicant interrupted interview to phone her therapist for advice on how to answer specific interview questions.

- Candidate brought large dog to interview.

- Applicant refused to sit down and insisted on being interviewed standing up.

- Candidate dozed off during the interview.

PLEASE DEPOSIT

ALL WORK IN TRAY

IT'S THE CIRCULAR RECEPTACLE UNDER MY DESK MARKED TRASH

Tricks to Liven up a Meeting

1. Spill coffee on the conference table. Produce a little paper boat and sail it down the table.

2. During a meeting, each time the boss makes an important point, (or at least one he/she seems to consider important), make a little noise like you are building up to an orgasm.

3. Stand up and act indignant. Demand that the boss tell you the 'real' reason this meeting has been called.

4. Give a broad wink to someone else at the table. In time, wink at everyone. Sometimes shake your head just a little, as if to indicate that the speaker is slightly crazy and everybody knows it.

5. When there is a call for questions, lean back in your chair, prop your feet up on the table, smile contentedly, and say, "Well, here's the way I see it, J.B..." (or any other impressive-sounding initials that are not actually your boss's.)

6. Bring a small mountain of computer printouts to the meeting. If possible, include some old-fashioned fanfold paper for dramatic effect. Every time the speaker makes a point, pretend to check it in one of the printouts. Pretend to find substantiating evidence there. Nod vigorously, and say 'uh-huh, uh-huh!'

7. Bring a hand puppet, preferably an animal. Ask it to clarify difficult points.

8. Arrange to have a poorly-dressed young woman with an infant quietly enter the meeting, stare directly at the speaker for a while, burst into tears, then leave the room.

9. Complain loudly that your neighbour won't stop touching you. Demand that the boss make him/her stop doing it.

10. Stay behind as everyone else, including the boss, leaves. Thank them for coming.

PROBLEMS AND COMPLAINTS THAT WAY

Murphy's Laws at Work

Important letters that contain no errors will develop errors in the mail.

The last person that quit or was fired will be the one held responsible for everything that goes wrong - until the next person quits or is fired.

There is never enough time to do it right the first time, but there is always enough time to do it over.

The more pretentious a corporate name, the smaller the organization. (For instance, The Murphy Center for Codification of Human and Organizational Law, contrasted to IBM, GM, AT&T ...).

If you are good, you will be assigned all the work. If you are really good, you will get out of it.

You are always doing something marginal when the boss drops by your desk.

People are always available for work in the past tense.

If it wasn't for the last minute, nothing would get done.

At work, the authority of a person is inversely proportional to the number of pens that person is carrying.

OUT TO LUNCH

and short

of a sandwich

Great humorous lines from office employee evaluations

1. I would not allow this employee to breed.

2. This associate is not so much of a has-been, but more definitely a won't-be.

3. Works well when under constant supervision and cornered like a rat in a trap.

4. **When she opens her mouth, it seems it is only to change whatever foot was previously there.**

5. This young lady has delusions of adequacy.

6. **He set low personal standards and then consistently fails to achieve them.**

7. This employee is depriving a village somewhere of an idiot.

8. **This employee should go far, and the sooner he starts, the better.**

9. Got into the gene pool while the lifeguard was not looking.

10. **Got a full 6-pack, but lacks the plastic thing to hold it together.**

11. A photographic memory but with the lens cover glued on.

12. **A prime candidate for natural de-selection.**

13. If you give him a penny for his thoughts, you will get change.

14. **If you stand close enough to him, you can hear the ocean.**

15. Since my last report, this employee has reached rock bottom and has started to dig.

TELL ME
WHAT YOU NEED

And I'll tell you how to get along without it

Managing Editor: Simon Melhuish
Editor: Nikole G Bamford

Designed and compiled by
Loncraine Broxton
PO Box 311, KT2 5QW, UK
PO Box 990676, Boston, MA 02199, USA

ISBN: 1904797334

www.thelagoongroup.com

Printed in China